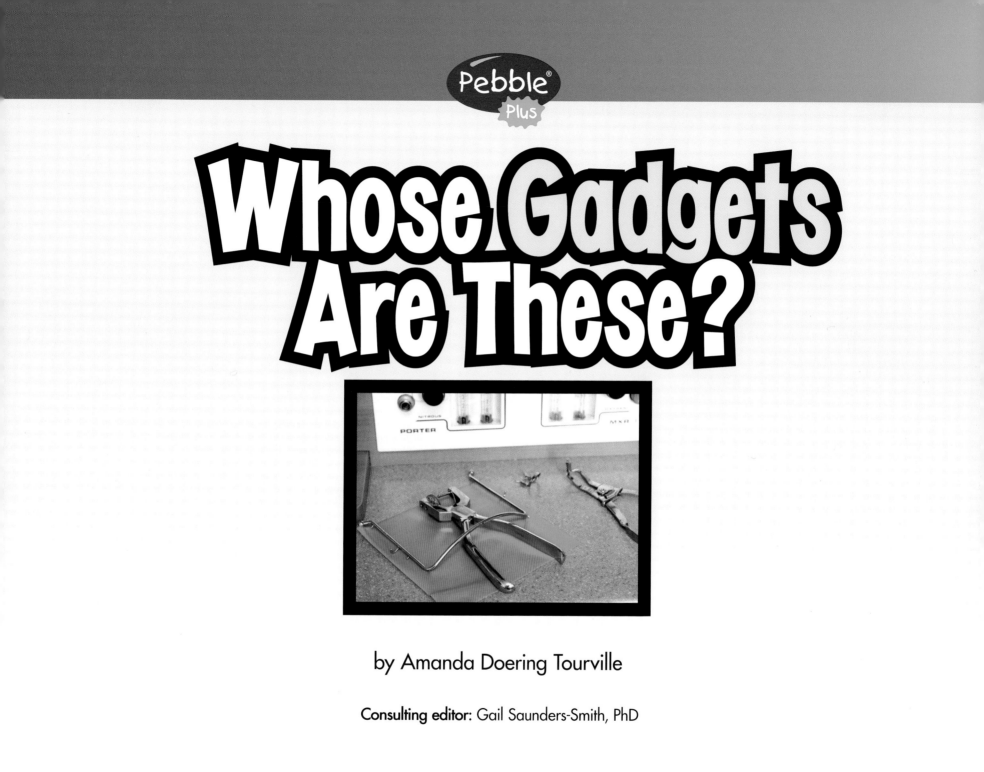

Pebble® Plus

Whose Gadgets Are These?

by Amanda Doering Tourville

Consulting editor: Gail Saunders-Smith, PhD

CAPSTONE PRESS
a capstone imprint

Pebble Plus is published by Capstone Press,
151 Good Counsel Drive, P.O. Box 669, Mankato, Minnesota 56002.
www.capstonepub.com

Books published by Capstone Press are manufactured with paper
containing at least 10 percent post-consumer waste.

Library of Congress Cataloging-in-Publication Data
Tourville, Amanda Doering, 1980–
  Whose gadgets are these? / by Amanda Doering Tourville.
    p. cm.—(Pebble plus books. Community helper mysteries)
  Includes bibliographical references and index.
  Summary: "Simple text and full-color photographs present a mystery community helper, one clue at a time,
until his or her identity is revealed"—Provided by publisher.
  ISBN 978-1-4296-6082-2 (library binding)
  1. Dentists—Juvenile literature. 2. Dentistry—Juvenile literature. I. Title. II. Series.
  RK63.T684 2012
  617.6092—dc22   2011005505

Editorial Credits
Jeni Wittrock, editor; Matt Bruning and Bobbie Nuytten, designers; Wanda Winch, media researcher;
    Laura Manthe, production specialist; Sarah Schuette, photo stylist; Marcy Morin, photo scheduler

Photo Credits
All photos by Capstone Studio/Karon Dubke except:
Shutterstock: Flavio Massari, 19, mypokcik, puzzle design element

Capstone would like to thank Associates in Oral Surgery Ms for the use of their office space for this book.

Note to Parents and Teachers

The Community Helper Mysteries set supports social studies standards related to communities.
This book describes and illustrates dentists. The images support early readers in understanding
the text. The repetition of words and phrases helps early readers learn new words. This book
also introduces early readers to subject-specific vocabulary words, which are defined in the
Glossary section. Early readers may need assistance to read some words and to use the Table of
Contents, Glossary, Read More, Internet Sites, and Index sections of the book.

Printed in the United States of America in North Mankato, Minnesota.

122011   006514R

Table of Contents

It's a Mystery

This book is full of clues
about me. I am a helper
in your community.
Can you guess what I do?

Here's your first clue: I work
in an office.

Gadgets I Use

I use mirrors in my work.

The mirrors help me to see

into small, dark places.

I also use sharp, pointy, metal tools. They help me poke around to find bad spots.

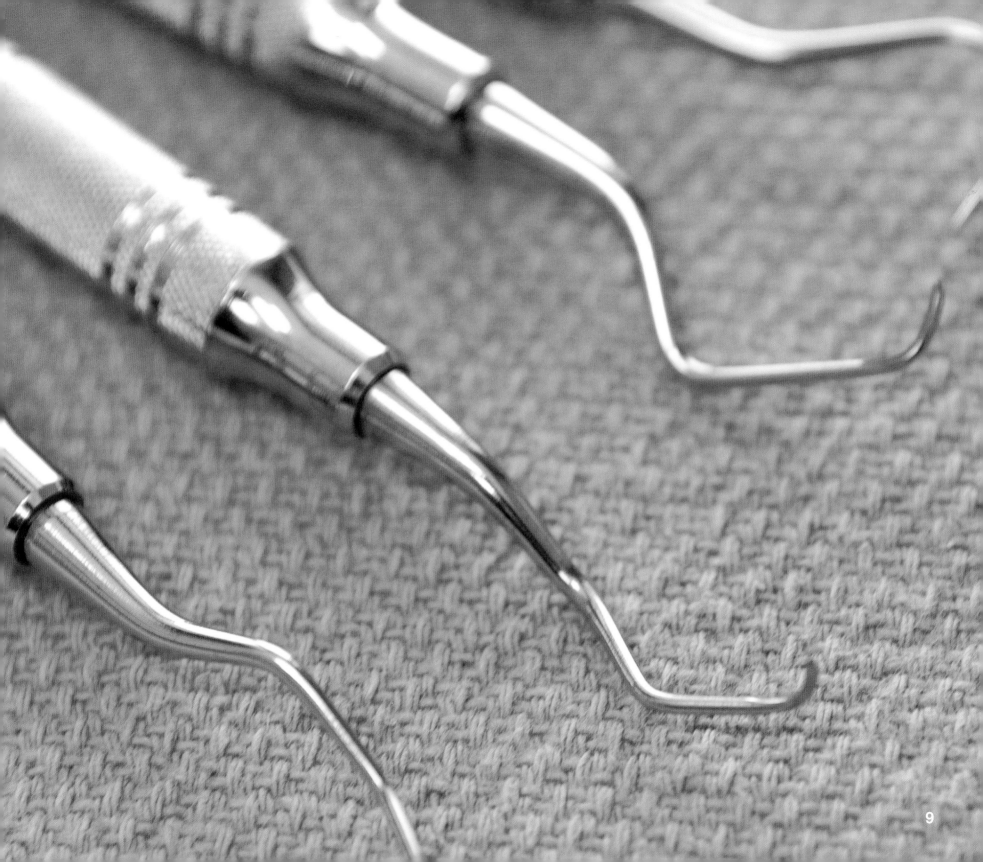

A special chair helps me
do my job. This chair goes up
and down. You can lie down
or sit up in this chair.

What I Wear

I wear gloves to protect us both. Germs can't get through my gloves.

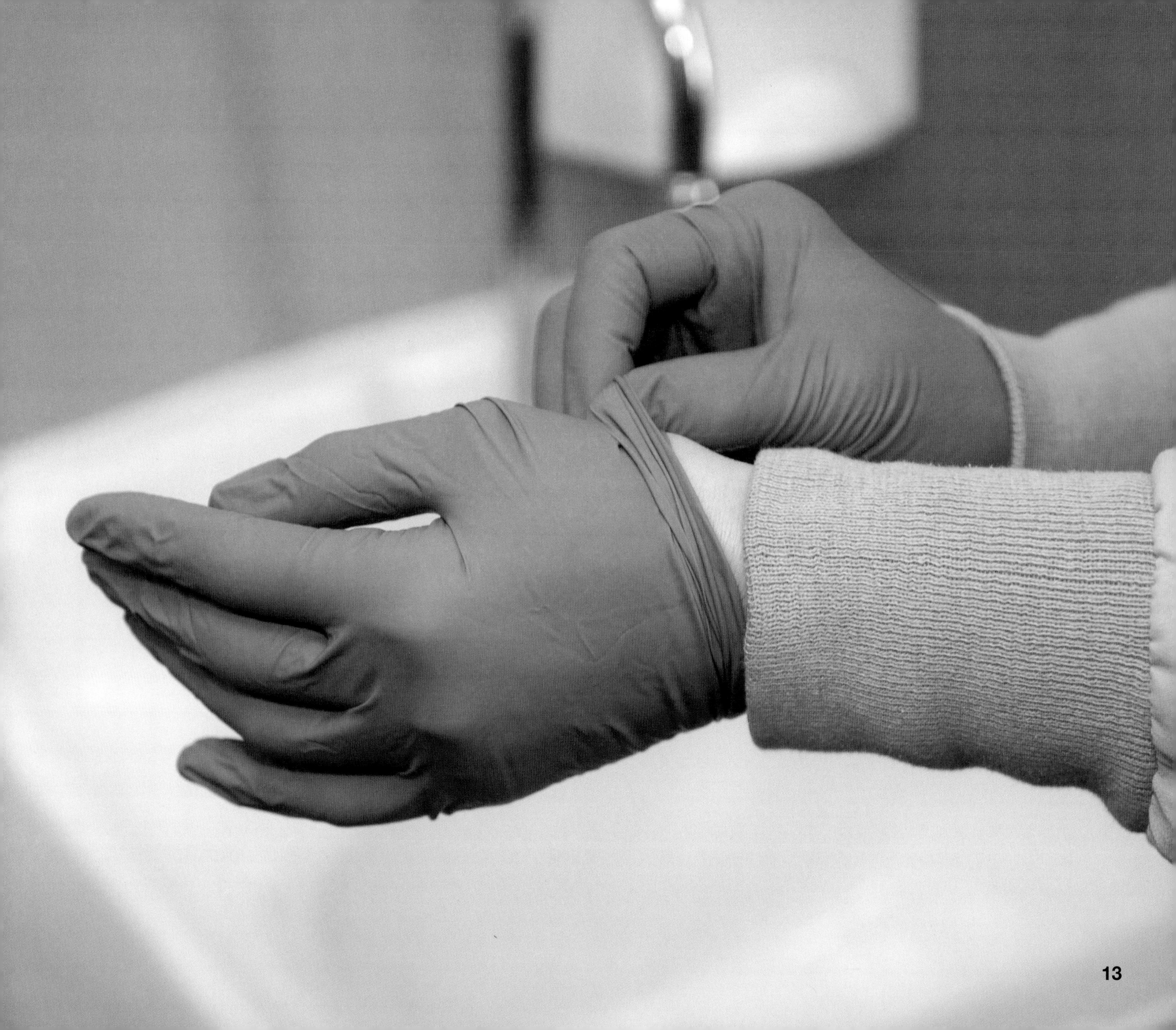

I wear a coat over my clothes.
I also wear a mask over my
nose and mouth. Safety glasses
protect my eyes.

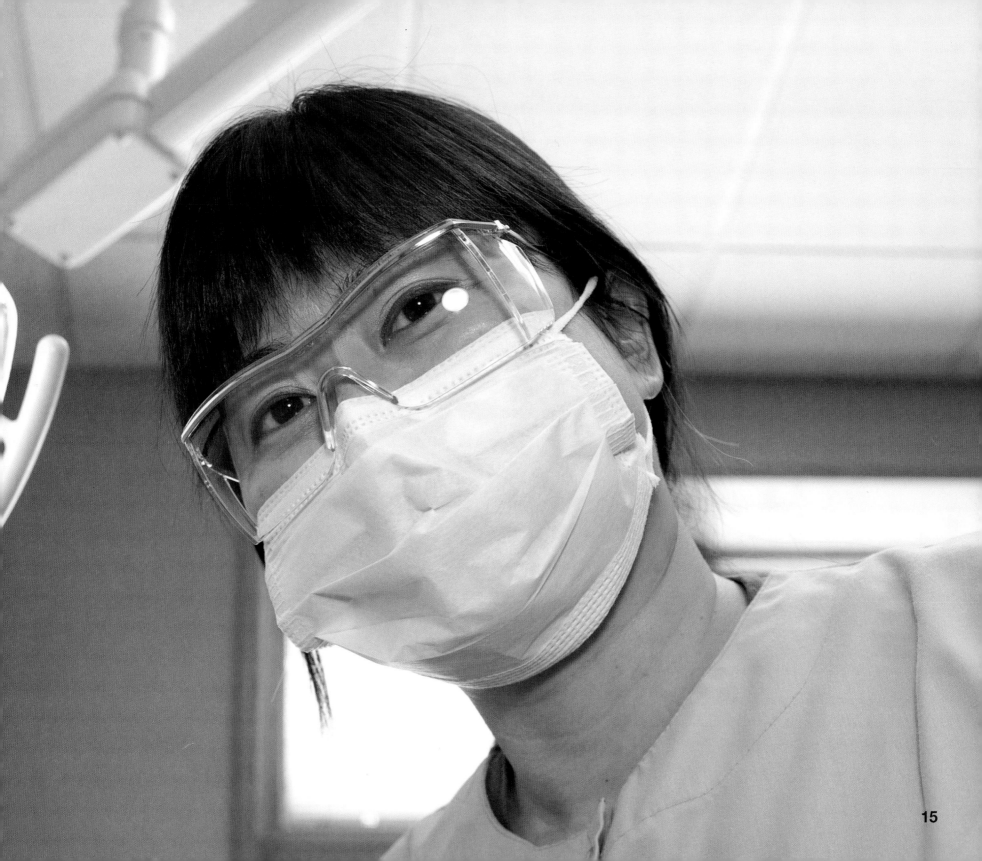

How I Can Help

I look over one part
of your body. I patch holes
and cracks to help keep
you healthy and strong.

Does your smile have a problem?

I might use a special drill to fix it.

Have you guessed who I am?

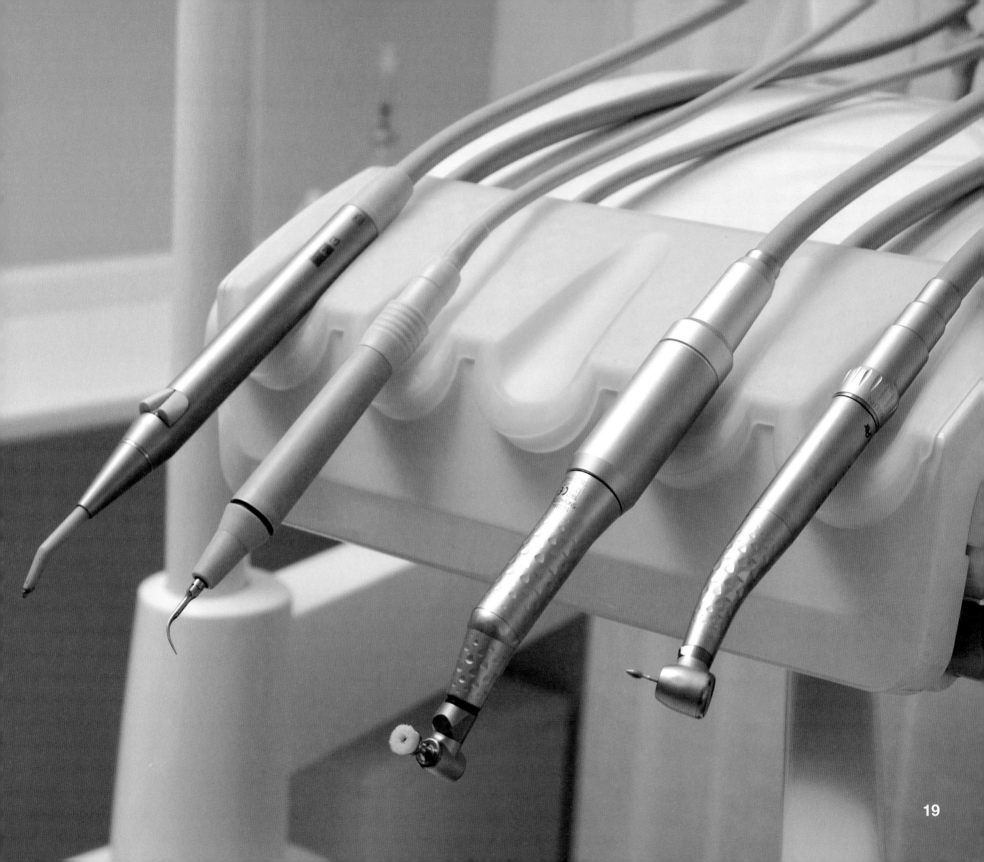

Mystery Solved!

I'm a dentist!

This community helper mystery
is solved.

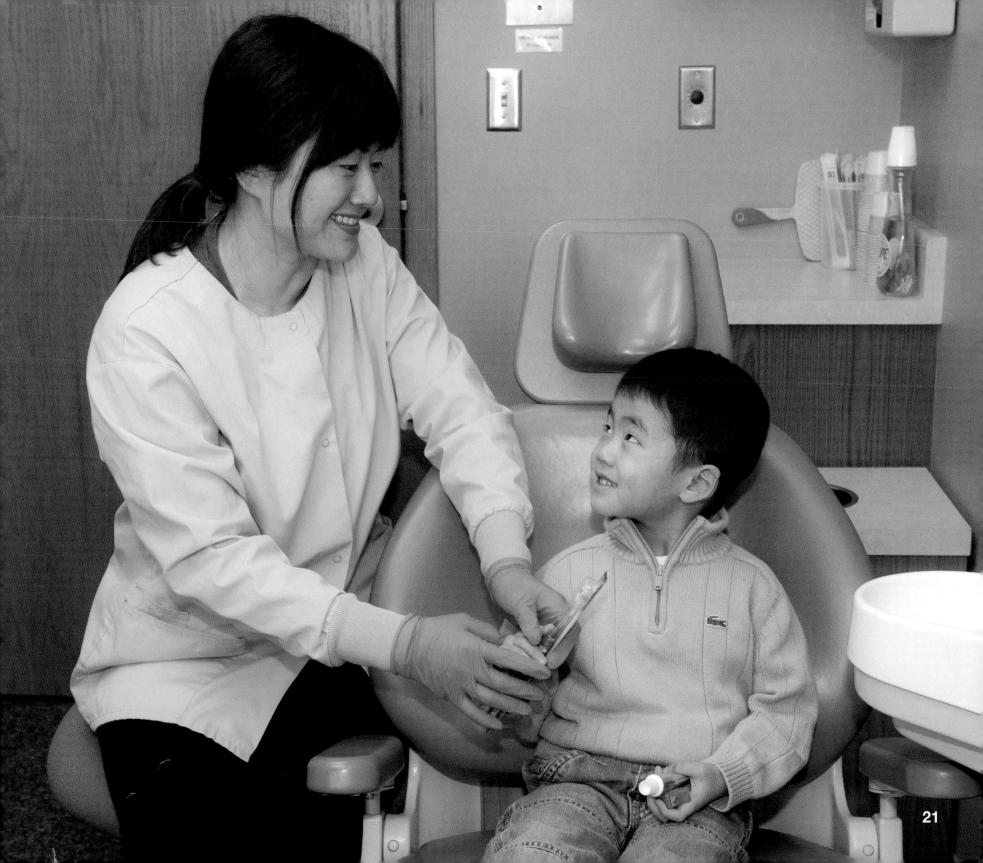

Glossary

germ—a very small living organism that can cause disease

office—a room or building in which people work, usually sitting at desks

patch—to fix or fill in a hole or weak spot

protect—to guard or keep safe from harm

Read More

Crabtree, Marc. *Meet My Neighbor, the Dentist.* Meet My Neighbor. New York: Crabtree Pub., 2010.

Gillis, Jennifer B. *Neighborhood Helpers.* My Neighborhood. Vero Beach, Fla.: Rourke Pub., 2007.

Schuh, Mari. *At the Dentist.* Healthy Teeth. Mankato, Minn.: Capstone Press, 2008.

Internet Sites

FactHound offers a safe, fun way to find Internet sites related to this book. All of the sites on FactHound have been researched by our staff.

Here's all you do:

Visit *www.facthound.com*

Type in this code: 9781429660822

Check out projects, games and lots more at
www.capstonekids.com

Index

Word Count: 171
Grade: 1
Early-Intervention Level: 13